TODD AND HIS INNER CRITTER CRITIC NAMED CREED

Written by Stephanie Todd, LCSW

Illustrated by Amanda Letcher

For Grandpa, whose passion for storytelling sparked my own, and whose wisdom and love remain with me always. Love and miss you.

And for Mom, who brings stories to life with her art, just as she did for Grandpa's book. Love you mama bear!

On a snowy mountain peak
where the air was crisp and clear,
lived an adventurous fox named Todd,
who loved to race down the slopes,
always smiling ear to ear.

Todd loved to snowboard down the mountain, with a passion so true.
He dreamed of performing all sorts of tricks and flips, ever since he was two!

At just two years old, Papa Fox
took Todd to a Snowboard Trick Show,
where Todd watched pro snowboarders
like Lando the Llama perform
TRICKS AND FLIPS in the snow!

From that day forward,
Todd had a dream,
a daring feat to try.

He wanted to perform a backflip
on his snowboard so he could

SOAR THROUGH THE SKY!

Then one chilly day,
Todd stood atop a steep hill.
His snowboard strapped on, paws
planted firm, he was ready for the thrill.

When deep in his mind appeared
his Inner Critter Critic named Creed,
a voice of self-doubt who would
PLANT SELF-DOUBT SEEDS.

Inner Critic Creed whispered,

"Backflips are tricky, Todd.
YOU'RE BOUND TO FALL.

You're not skilled enough,
DON'T ATTEMPT IT AT ALL!"

Todd's heart felt heavy, his spirit grew weak.
Creed's words echoed loudly,
making it hard for Todd to speak.

But deep down inside, Todd heard a faint voice from Lando the Llama, who whispered,

"Don't give up, Todd!
YOU HAVE THE CHOICE!

The choice to keep trying, to be brave and face fears, to celebrate your small wins, to be LOUD in your cheers!"

Todd took a deep breath,
steadied himself,
ready to take flight.

He LAUNCHED
into the air,

SPINNING HARD
with all his might.

But fear crept into his mind,
and doubts began to grow.
His body froze mid-flip,
and then WHAAAAM!

He face-planted into the snow!

Dejected and disheartened,
Todd began to cry.
When someone from
behind him whispered,

"COME ON,
KID. GIVE IT
ANOTHER TRY!"

Todd turned and saw a
snow-carving highland cow.

The cow gave Todd two thumbs up
and said, "Keep practicing, bro!
And don't forget to enjoy the

POW!"

Todd paused for a moment as he sat in the snow,
breathing in the crisp air, slowly letting his worries go.

He embraced the stillness, the beauty all around,
grateful for this moment of calmness he had found.

Then Todd sought out his friends,
Albie the Alpaca and Geo the Giraffe,
who gave Todd some wise advice.

They said, "Believe in yourself and
practice. Then, go for it, Todd!
DON'T THINK TWICE!"

They built a small jump in Geo's backyard,
a place to practice and improve.

With each try, Todd grew stronger
as he got into the groove.

"PAUSE and BREATHE,"
said Albie, "Give doubt a little space.
Replace it with affirmations,
and let positivity take doubt's place."

Geo added, "Visualize success, Todd.
See yourself land with pride.
Your Inner Critic Creed will fade,
and your higher self will guide!"

Encouraged by his friends,
Todd climbed up the mountain peak
with newfound determination and a
PRACTICED NEW TECHNIQUE.

With a burst of energy,
Todd sped down the slope,
launching into the air,
a heart full of hope.

When AGAIN, Creed still lingered,
trying to bring him down,
Todd took a deep breath,
determined to stand his ground.

He said,
"Thank you, Creed, for your cautious voice.
I know you're just trying to protect me.
But I'm going to go for it, I've got this!
THIS IS MY MOMENT TO SOAR,
JUST WATCH ME!"

Todd acknowledged the
doubt and then let it go.
He replaced it with self-confidence,
allowing his abilities to just flow.

He then FLiPPED gracefully,
his spirit soaring HiGH.

His determination SHINING like a beacon in the sky!

In that brief moment, time seemed to freeze.
as Todd NAILED the backflip, with skill and perfect ease!

Todd landed with a smile, greeted by cheers so grand.
Creed's voice fell silent, realizing he's no longer in command.

It was in that moment, on that snowy peak so high,
Todd showed the world that even

FOXES CAN FLY!

So, my friends, remember, when self-doubt appears,
you've got what it takes to overcome all your fears!

Embrace your courage, let your true story unfold,
FOR WITHIN YOU LIES A STRENGTH
MUCH MORE PRECIOUS THAN GOLD.

Four Inner Critter Critic Exercises:

1 Ask your child to name their inner critic:

This may sound silly, but it helps your child separate the words and actions of the inner critic from their own. This gives them a better chance of taming harsh criticisms and unhelpful thoughts that eventually build into habits of rumination. It doesn't matter what they call their inner critic, (I call mine Seth don't ask me why) just as long as it makes sense to them. It can also help to externalize the inner critic by drawing it on paper.

2 Take the BFF test:

You might notice the inner critic creeping around your child on tough days. They start being really hard on themselves — "It's all my fault we lost the game." When you spot this ask them: "Would you speak like this to your best friend?" If the answer is "no," it's time to squash that negative self-talk, and encourage them to be their own BFF. Ask them to think about what they would say to a friend in a similar position, and also HOW they would say it. Regularly practicing this exercise will help them to take responsibility for their actions whilst also building self- compassion.- credit Dr. Hazel Harrison

3 ANSWER BACK:

You may spend a lot of time encouraging your child not to answer back, but when it comes to the inner critic, they need to boss them back. When you notice the inner critic sneakily chanting to them, "You are going to fail," "What if you mess up," encourage them to answer back. Use these sentences to help them fight back!

"That's enough out of you, inner critic!
I'm doing my best and that is good enough! Kick rocks!"

"I can't hear you, inner critic! I'm too busy being awesome over here."

4 CREATE "GLIMMER" MOMENTS EACH AND EVERY DAY.:

It can be tough when the inner critic has a megaphone and is yelling in your child's ear. It can make kids question themselves and their abilities. To cope with this relentless criticism, it's important that kids find things about themselves that they like. Each day, help your child find time to notice positive and neutral things about themselves. Encouraging a daily gratitude practice is a great way to build resilience, self-compassion, and to keep the inner critic quiet!

Loved this read? Don't miss out on Todd's first book!
Todd's Mindful Adventure is available on Amazon.

Made in United States
Troutdale, OR
10/01/2024

23307994R00021